Natural Trouble

Natural Trouble

SCOTT HIGHTOWER

FORDHAM UNIVERSITY PRESS
New York
2003

Library of Congress Cataloging-in-Publication Data

Hightower, Scott.
    Natural trouble / Scott Hightower.—1st ed.
      p. cm.
    ISBN 0-8232-2285-3 (hard cover : alk. paper)—ISBN
0-8232-2286-1
(pbk. : alk. paper)
I. Title.
PS3608.I37N38 2003
811'.54—dc21
2003005545

Printed in the United States of America
07 06 05 04 03   5 4 3 2 1
First Edition

For Jose and Tani

Do these buttons that we wear attest that our allegiance is to Nature?

—Captain Vere

God bless Captain Vere!

—Billy Budd

Contents

Grateful acknowledgments to the editors of the following publications, in which these poems first appeared, sometimes in earlier versions:

Callaloo: "Amazing Grace"
Columbia, A Magazine of Poetry and Prose: "Spring Shearing," "'52 Maneuvers"
Global City Review: "Salgado's *Two Men in a Sauna*"
Harvard Gay & Lesbian Review: "Fortune Three"
Hellas: "Tartessos"
The James White Review: "April 11, 1861, Arrowhead"
Lit: "Off the Hook," "Yasumasa Morimura as Frida Kahlo"
Phoebe: "Village Cena"
Ploughshares: "Caravaggio Moderno"
Quarterly West: "Mene, Mene, Tekel, Upharsin"
Poetry after 9/11: "Tontine"
Salmagundi: "St. Jerome and the Angel"
Southwest Review: "With an Instinctive Certainty of Charms of the Modish, 'For the Fairest'"
St. Luke's Review: "In Visiting Hours"
West Branch: "Dim Sum in Philadelphia," "Home Demonstration" (one of the sections of "Natural Trouble")
Yale Review: "Cusp and Tether"

Natural Trouble

Andean Serenade
at Santiago de Compostela

They are far from their mountains. Their music resists
    The advance of an ordinary night.
Has this faint, gray, mountain evening chill
    Of moist cloud and late lush green
        Followed them to this place?

Here between the granite columns and arches
    We, too, stand. Or, is it us
The mysterious vista has followed here this time,
    Instead of to one of our older, familiar
        Haunts of lovely Chaouen,

San Roque, Marrakesh, Mahabaleshwar,
    Or Katmandu? An occasional pilgrim's
Shell is cameoed on the outside sidewalk
    Portico above the exquisite
        Granite walk. Here,

Local and foreign, we congregate listening
    To the music. For the moment,
It is sufficient. For the moment, it
    Is the only protection any of us
        Feel we truly need.

Peas Porridge in the Pot

Each wheel wedge, outlined and labeled
in a light pencil print, separates
each of the seven arrangements made
from black-and-white and colored pictures
of foods cut from piles of old magazines.

Mom read *Prevention*; listened
to the early morning radio broadcast
with Dad. They drank blond
coffee and ate homemade
peach preserves on toast.

   *

Days have turned into decades
and a freak spring storm
has mauled our valley.
I phone to hear how things are.
"If you're looking for shade,
don't come to the ranch 'cause
there's not a leaf left on a tree."
Another parching summer, my mother
got right to the point: "Oh, Darlin',
we're livin' in a burnin' land."

   *

Is there ever going to be anything more elegant
than the shape lips and hands made
when we talked of our lives on the land?
Going to be anything more beautiful
than the catalog of sounds *that* world

made slipping into each day's morning,
each day's night?

My grandfather was a rancher
with a Dutch last name.
His ranch joined ours.
He read the *Baptist Standard*
and *Progressive Farmer,*
followed wool and mohair
prices, and listened to
the dry cattle market report.

At different times, each had
helped me with the India ink.
Now, clear Pennsylvania
Dutch egg noodle bags
parade the bright cartoon
of a rooster. Each has
a handy food pyramid printed
on its back . . . and jar labels
are covered with tiny
words and photographs.

Five Weather the Storm

Today's snow whirls down like a silent conqueror,
traces flurries surely mysterious to the early ancients.
All landmarks blur and try to make their edges
known, like issues argued in a patent war,
or roses in a drift of snow: two distant, pale,
veiled towers of silver; a fugitive streak of green.

Behavior, like light, like a particle, like a wave,
sinks into the shade the way crushed trees
sink to darkness. Carbon. Now there's
a topic for an aesthetic conversation.

Together, our friends speak in their native languages
of clinical emergencies in their countries
while I study the light. Not Hopper's,
Caravaggio's, or Monet's, but the one originating
on the other side of the entry's dark, translucent
glass above the frosted transom. You are thinking
of all the art we saw today. You suspect
none of us understood. The saxophonist
starts her riffs. I have been lazy. I deploy
a smile; and, together with the others,
we slip beyond the concrete.

Weather in Richard Long's Sculpture

> In its poetry and economy, *Walking*
> *in Circles* goes straight to the point.
> > —Peter Plagens, *Newsweek* magazine, 1991,
> > in a review of a Richard Long exhibition.

The unexpected intrusion   in the polite gallery
is not random, rather   is deployed according
to rules. Real   fragments of the landscape
(gorgeously Paleolithic)   assembled evoke
the inevitable parch   of clear mornings
and the release   of nights. Odd,
how together, these sentinels   comprise a glyphless
catalog of flowering   color and loss.

Take It Away

So we beat on, boats against the current,
borne back ceaselessly into the past.
                    —F. Scott Fitzgerald, *The Great Gatsby*

Very late some nights, I have seen at one
of the windows in the tall building across
the street one of my anonymous neighbors
come to the window to smoke cigarettes.
I have watched, not out of prurient interest,
but with the notion that someone else might
have just laid down a novel about the Fitzgeralds,
that tonight, besides me, someone else
might be considering the notion
of a desolate country without frontiers.

In 1929, Marianne Moore moved
to Brooklyn and Diaghilev died in Venice.

The Fitzgerald marriage at the rectory
of St. Patrick's Cathedral in New York
and the Biltmore Hotel honeymoon
had already collapsed into a series
of matrimonial bouts and the emotional
turmoil of the age. Two fanciful imaginations
were already fatalistically locked
in a malevolent *folie à deux*. We carry
our clarity, frenetic squalor, or doom with us
wherever we go. "A place is what you make it."

Growing self-possession makes one a student
of affectation, a student of the sophomoric,

6

the trashy, stupid risks; keen to the boast
of escape. Fitzgerald, himself tragically insightful,
called Hollywood "a tragic city of beautiful girls."

It was said of Zelda, "She wants to be told
what she is like, being too young to know
that she is like nothing at all."
The obligation is, after all, with the people
who understand remedy, at some point,
becomes an impossible situation.

Eventually it would not be her husband,
but other women who brought a semblance
of stability to Zelda Fitzgerald's life.
In the end, she would conform
to her mother's garden and steal herself
to face her husband's funeral alone.

> *the raucous delirium: those delirious parties*
> *. . . on the verge of nervous exhaustion*
> *. . . enveloped in tragedy and pursued by a doom*
> *general aimlessness and boredom*
> *desperation in the mood behind it*
> *strained and even hysterical*
> *. . . sureness that you are righter than anyone else*
> *grotesque intensity*
> *In the end, are Europe's cities as empty*
>   *and tiresome as America's small towns?*
> *. . . to stimulate creativity, assuage self-doubt,*
> *mollify loneliness, and bolster self-confidence*
> *"Life seemed so uselessly extravagant"*

like the band leader who turns to his orchestra
and jubilates the imperative, "Take it away!"

or the television host who—pausing
for a commercial break in the telecast—
tells the guest, "Don't go away!"

or the people that built a glistening city.
When barbarians attacked and toppled
the beautiful towers, those same people
turned to their strongest and ablest
men and women and said to them,
"Sift through the rubble and take it away."

Tontine

May 23, 1864

At Pemigewasset House
Pierce and Hawthorne took adjoining rooms and slept
    with the connecting
          door ajar. A dog's
    bark stirred the ex-president from his
      sleep, but—"in the twinkling of
an eye"—not the other weary traveler.
    Sumner wrote to Longfellow,
        "One by one,
almost in twos, they seem to go."

'52 Maneuvers

For how long do brothers
share the inheritance?

—*Epic of Gilgamesh*, Tablet X

Texas. June, 1952. The twentieth-century
world, already separated into two great vats
of darkness, was already militarized.
Just a hundred years earlier, some
had tried camels on the western plains.
Now, Fort Hood ran maneuvers
through the fences and across
the terraces of our charge, the land.

Instead of cutting his fences
in the middle of the spans—where repairs
would have been simplest to make—
they "took out" whole corners.
My father watched them. I have often
wondered how he must have felt:
the work undone, the work ahead.

From time to time, we would plow up
corroded relics of that week: a long black core,
a broken green-handled knife, fragments
of a helmet, canteen caps with chains.

My mother and my grandmother baked
pies; recalled the northern boys,
who couldn't tell goat from lamb,
asked for "berry pies."
They bayoneted coconut,

10

chocolate, banana cream; pooled
their money and split pies.

My father filled their orders;
delivered all of them warm
from the running boards and fenders
of his truck. That week, they kept
the ovens going late into the night;
long enough to bake out 465.

The old garden fence escaped
the clumsy maneuvers, but not
the competition or convenience
of the renovated grocery store in town.
The low tin roof of the old sheep shed
no longer serves as slide.
The dipping vat has grown
mysterious with vines.
The old tool shed has given way.

My sister was the first to leave.
She married a local boy turned
soldier. They started their family
in a nearby town. My beloved
brother went off to sew a few
wild oats before he settled down.
I was the one that left
to get an education.

The hapless soldiers left in June.
Early August, I wrangled out
into the brutal tontine—
the family's greedy child.

Village Cena

In the dark, high above the barkeep's head,
the gently swinging, mirrored prom ball
doesn't rotate. Mexican. Disco. Votives
flicker. *Banditos Ditto* in orange neon
shivers across the bar's mirror. Caravaggio:
all the customers, paired and turning, zigzag
into each other. Your *moros y cristianos*
gives us both pause. The limy margaritas—
with salt rimming the stemmed glasses—look
like white heaps of frozen terrain, glittery
new terra firma.
                    The world is an unstable place.
These days the fabric too often is ragged
down to a single desk, a bed, a Roman cell.
We discuss society, some of the complexities
of finding common abstract ground, concrete
atrocities, and how throughout the ages
tribal bloodlines have reared children,
filled mass graves, fueled "ethnic cleansing."
The restaurant feels safe and luxurious.

Caravaggio Moderno

David with the Head of Goliath, 1609–1610?

No bronze, paraphernalia, or feathers.
No euphoric cheers or parade. Simply
The slayer and his prey. The boy's body
Shines horrific as a candle. Without
Tenderness, the light cuts his skin
Across the arm; around a nipple; his chest
And neck; across the wrinkles of his brow,
His solemn and resilient lips: washed,
Still, unkissed. The light avails us down
To the youth's fist. From its clench, the giant's
Damaged wall-eyed head hangs unadored.

St. Jerome and the Angel

Jusepe de Ribera, 1626

It's not as though the subject has just come up.
Somewhere between you and the airborne angel,

wind that does not merely trumpet demise;
in the horror of his music clearly

the theme . . . no . . . the problem of what to do
with blood and meat resonates in your skin,

your shape: Desire as old as
—or older than—flesh itself.

"What shall we say then? Is the law sin?
God forbid. Nay, I had not known sin, but by the law."

Yes, we know how Paul continued
that the commandment was ordained

to life and he,
being mortal, to death.

Augustine with his "importune
and nefarious desires"

and you with your (it has been said)
rebellious member par excellence—

scrolled to Paul and read:
"The law is spiritual: but I am carnal."

Ribera, here, has lit you with a radiance,
uncharacteristically has thrown open

your arms, your face,
your hands—like butterflies.

Here, your whole swathed reaching
dappled verticality appears to be begging, "Where

should I be employed? Where would you have me turn
in this ever-rising palimpsest of crime and world?"

Natural Trouble

Our teacher hands us a sheet of paper and tells us
to draw what we most want to be when we grow up.

The big *u* is the universal base
of my earless head. For feet—ankles and feet
are not easy—chunky black shoes
will suffice. The "missionary" wears
a blue suit, a necktie. A bright red
theatrical curtain scallops across the top
and drapes down either flank of the page.
I only know missionaries are travelers—
like Lottie Moon whose work in China
we commemorate every Christmas.
Every man, one mission: from the gandy dancer
to Shiva. Fringed hammocks, sunbonnets,
cotton wagons, and summer watermelon
to library books about silk,
prosody, and counterpoint.
Dowsing rods to the conductor of *Turandot's*
orchestra pit and baton;
"Whistling Dick" and karaoke
to notions of justice and divine estate.

        *

    I wish; I want; if, then;
        and then there could be

    all the dreams:
so many reeking the suppositional.

———————
"Whistling Dick"—American slang for "a cannon."

I suppose there are different manners
of civilly floating

around our autographs of courage and fear,
the mercy seat:

from visions of being eaten alive
to a vision of living without a king.

                    *

My guess is that neither prayer nor taxes
will repair the left arm of the statue.
Late fall, late spring: the student
is there with a book list,
two of my conscientious colleagues,
and me. Glimpsing out the window
at two pairs of sunlit reposing cornice
statues hovering over the tenth-floor windows
across the street, I wonder about
the left arm of one of the statues.

                    *

My mother followed my advice
and served a pudding and a trifle
marbled with custard, pineapple,
coconut, and a layer of cream
whipped to the texture of satin.
I watched her lead a circle of other young
wives of ranchers—all her old familiarities
amplified: clean, curled, and wrinkle-
free; her signature red lipstick.
Frankly, I found the prim platter of crustless,
ladyfinger sandwiches—tuna salad,
cucumber, pimento cheese—a bit queer.

I was, however, impressed with her:
"Rather than fill each glass from the tap,
fill the pitcher and then pour from *it*
into your glasses. That way, you conserve
your energy." I could see for myself,
besides modern and efficient,
that she was also generous
and good. Yes. Very, very good.

                    *

On occasion, we hung antlered deer
        and, more routinely, pigs
from trees. Ahead, without clouds
        of steam, the smell of burning
wood, and the shifting of coals
        beneath roiling pots,
would be the goats draining
        from clearer, smaller trees.
One of my first jobs was the dull
        encompassing tub,
galvanized vault,
        and the nervous bird,
which—in thrusting out its
        neck—accommodated
my axe. There was also a prized
        mare I knew as beautiful
before I knew the songs of
        Old World thrushes.
I helped my father hobble her,
        then we watched as
a neighbor's sun-bright stallion
        stained her with his lathery,
gravy-colored semen.

        At our small-town church,
we gathered to address

18

the cardinal myths
of secrets, burdens, and cause.
    There was the original
dreamer, gardener, and architect;
    a word and a fountain
filled with blood.

    Our backs were turned
on the Native American
    and irreversibly on Rome.

My imagination,
    fostered, romped
through a mosaic field
    of iconographic Israel,
Greece, and Europe, a field
    of patriarchal opportunities,

and (as I was a boy)
    of power,
through which, if approached
    with an orthodox interpretation,
life could unfold as an almost
    endless opening up.

I had my doubts.

    There was a shimmer
of something else (we either
    see or refuse to see),
another promise.
    As early as "Cowboys & Indians,"
"Doctor, and House," I sensed that
    some things might be
marbled through
    with the equal presence
of things as they are not.

19

In the bright motes
of a secluded saddle house,
    in the hands of a boy
just older than myself,
    I nervously began
asking why, in the end, all
    bodies must go forsaken.

Trouble Opening the Record

It was easy, surrounded
by a host of distant cousins,
to reverse the sequence, lose a sire.

Inheritance, connecting names,
generations, secrets, and silence:
youth rarely searches far up tributaries
of blood for illegitimacies, rarely
scours the turf of an elder's heart.

One sleeping dog beneath a mattress:
a delicate girl coupled
with a rougher neighbor family's son.
Trace: Christmas, 1901.

> *Had he egressed to war?*
> *Was he a traveler? Marked unworthy*
> *by her clan as kin?*
> *Engaged to someone else?*
> *Already a married man?*

We bury the secret one by one.

By the time I got around to bating
the numbers on stones, only
the retelling of one obscure oldtimer
might recall: someone nearly having
gotten killed; someone else seething
and whisking away his dogs
and daughter for a season.

Shortly after their return,
the persnickety young German

who lived on the adjoining place—
his lovely wife already untimely gone—
groomed himself a second time
(him, too, alone with a daughter)
for another wedding portrait.

Nowhere more clearly
than in a small town is love
love; an infidelity, a whisper,
a stone tossed deliberately
to rest on the floor of a local lake.

                    *

My grandmother's attachment to her mother
Seemed more than simple offspring loyalty.
Both women wore thin gold wedding bands
And wire-rimmed glasses. Her mother's life
Appeared simple: for years bedridden
And frail. She liked to read newspapers

And dip snuff. Her watery eyes,
Lens magnified, descended; reaching
Beyond the fragrance of roses and peonies
As she took the tribute of children's
Kisses. All that sun-drenched white,
The glowing hierophant's pale hands
Extending like canyons of blue veins.

Evil lurked at the edges of her house,
Obeyed a distance. Its barren reports
Loitered across the drafty entry hall,
Lingered where a blustering fir limb
Dragged itself across a window screen.

Great Grandpa shaved on the porch;
Changed in his lattice room, peculiar

Male sanctuary; split and stacked
Firewood, messed with ashes or the flue.
Eleven-elevenths husband; ten-elevenths
Father, and one-eleventh stepfather;
Though, it was not until all of them
Were dead that I began to crack the code.

Mysterious Real Estate

> . . . in sparkling dark
> a trail of a star & dies"
> —John Berryman, *Homage to Mistress Bradstreet*

I. "SELF"

The handmaiden or the body servant
holds up the pagan bronze or silver

and there it is: the insatiable bird
with a pair of plums, the pair

of tender apples appearing
backward in the shiny tray

or awkward mirror; each uncharted
gesture the authentic raiment of a risk.

II. "TIME"

The plains of solemnity and play
Attest to how a mortal ransom's
Paid for each profane affection.

Once, buccaneers elected to dangle
Gold from an ear, "Pay for another
To lay me to rest in sod." A stone lamb

Kneels marking a pair of graves.
Nearby, the descending crown of a marble
Hand blooms on a marble harp.

Carriage

The assassins that blow themselves
to bits with the same bomb they
use to snipe: "suicide bombers"?

The sleek journalistic formula "suicide bomber"
has so much slippage it can be read—on one hand—
"freedom fighter,"—on the other—"vicious sociopath."

What are we left to do with an epithet
that parades the epaulettes of nonjudgmental
information; but which—in actuality—
stops thought? And is there any decency
or fair play in deception? Doesn't turning oneself
into a mechanism of delivery and detonation
mean that one is actually a part
of the bomb? How and when exactly
was the moniker "ground zero" settled on?

Tullio Lombardo's *Adam* shattered
one evening at the Met,
collapsed of its own volition—

alone, like some pagan god
who, abandoned by his mortal
worshipers, threw himself on the floor
and smashed himself to bits.

The *conoscenti* had to collect and number
the pieces of marble strewn on the museum floor,
which was cordoned off by tape
and string like a crime scene:
arms and legs, a torso and a head. . . .

The features of the face suffered
only minor losses, mostly scratches.
One leg was broken into six large pieces.
Other parts had been smashed into smaller
bits. There was some pulverizing.

Besides its strong classical references,
the statue was noted for the purity
of its marble, its smooth carving,
and its elegant hand, which held an apple.
There was a serpent and a grapevine.

The Peaceable Kingdom
of the Branch

Edward Hicks, 1780–1849

No observer loiters in these framed estates.
Abundance spills and overwhelms with milk

and honey. The wolf, the bright-eyed leopard,
and the young lion—lying beside the lamb,

the kid, the calf, respectively, seem to say:
"No difference for the sake of difference.

What I do is me; for that I came
unpaid." For Hicks, each was a spreading

of the Quaker word. (He earned his dollars
painting signs and coaches.) Significant

collections across the country—from New York
to California—have acquired one.

Many are on public display. Originally,
each painting was a gift carefully tied

in a ribbon of beliefs and spoken words.
Where are those self-possessing eyes,

their scribbles and allusive smears?
Here, we are given pause that the tender

mounts around an innocent palm
are the only seals capable

of keeping that damned
tunneling cockatrice contained.

Rattle of Bones

This morning, the swarming sirens
of police cars and an ambulance
were the first things I heard.

       *

By the end of my schooling, I had read
La Belle Dame sans Merci, My Last Duchess,
Four Preludes on Playthings in the Wind,
The Waste Land and had had my fill
of that dreadful high school game,
"the brightest light bulb on the tree."
I had copied various aphorisms
into my notebook, things like
"at my back in a cold blast
I hear the rattle of the bones."

       *

SUFFERING SAPPHO

Don't kid yourself. It wasn't just a casual loss
or the anonymous ravages of time. The comics
of antiquity loved to buffoon Sappho, bard of Lesbos.
Aristophanes of Byzantium and Aristarchus of Samothrace
collected and edited her work into nine books.
(I know no ancient Greek at all.)
But years later, when scholars
began to transcribe works
from papyrus scrolls to bound books,
Sappho's work was not transcribed.

And, later still, her verses were among
the books burned in two Gregorian fires.

fragment 94: ". . . what suffering is ours!
For it is against my will that I leave you."

Who knows what she would have thought
of seeing someone like Madonna in cheap tabloids
or being lampooned on late-night television.
One can only imagine her grazing the sensational
headlines, the clearly intrusive—but titillating
photographs. "Inquiring minds want to know."

Who knows what she would have thought in 1897,
when archeologists in Egypt uncovered
her verses lining ancient coffins
or on scrumpled bunches of papyrus
contained within the stomachs
of mummified crocodiles.
(You can't make this stuff up!)
Her first modern collection
was published in 1925.
In December, 1941, "Suffering Sappho!"
Wonder Woman debuted. Ironically,
the defiant Amazon from a female Utopia
called Paradise Island (roughly based on San Francisco?)
was unable to prevent the invasion of Pearl Harbor.

*

DISTILLED SPIRITS

The Canadian geese have continued north.
It's spring and everywhere trees are flowering.
Even the shopping rows have gone ahead
and slipped into garish summer duds:

bright sheer dresses, cheap shoes, brightly colored sunshades;
artificial flowers and lingerie; rows of inexpensive toys.

       *

April. Almost into May. Inside the precinct
behind Collins Auditorium, two sentinels,
boisterous tulip trees, shoulder the gravel walk.
The pair litter the ground, like parading petalers
strewning the way for a triumphal entry.

gate   *   walk (gray gravel, gray granite) through
               the aisles of headstones   *
wall * hedge * evergreens

men of an order
laid out as they chose to live

The altar wall of red clay fired bricks
on a wall of cut gray granite stones
has two iron rings for . . . whatever . . . ,
a picket roof of twelve planks, and a top
ornament that looks like a monstrance:
Solomon's seal inside a circle, with a red
cabochon set in its center. Curling trefoils
radiating on the outside form a kind of cross.

The brand new stones are more symmetrical
and uniformed than the ones they replace.
A tiny cross is cut into the granite
at the top of each headstone legend;
each record: a name, a rank, three dates (bird
into the world, election to life in the order, birth
into the eternity beyond the world).
Three evergreens curl beyond the box border hedge.

Venezuela, Mexico, Cuba, Jamaica, Costa Rica
Kilkenny, Tipperary, Wicklow, Limerick, Wexford
Ghent and Ooteglem, Conrad, the Rhine
Savannah GA, Canton MA, Miners Mills PA
Caledonia, Wappingers Falls, Ogdensburg, Brooklyn
scholar, novice, diocesan seminarian, student
Jeremiah, David
Andrew, James, John, Thomas
Henry Charles Richard William George
Valentine and Patrick
Brother Desire

In the first row of the old cemetery,
there are thirteen original stones. One
is in the shape of a cross. Evidently,
at one time, it broke into two pieces
and had to be repaired. I, leaving,
take note of its missing one arm.

Swan Eaters

A poem is like a piece of fruit;
when it is ready, it will fall.

—Mallarmé

On the window sill of my hotel room, four
Water-filled plastic sentinels mark the harmonic
center of tourist order: pale sapphire,
aspic topaz, orange, byzantine green.

I've stared at them, around them, through them at two
rattling palm trees and an Umbrian terrace swathed
in wisteria. The ramshackle temple is curtained
with a line of laundry. I have stared at them
before a day trip to the synagogue
in Florence, the gilded church in Trastevere.

I often join my thirsty comrades on "our" terrace.
We have cooed over postcards (Giotto's
St. Francis Preaching to the Birds, Martini's
The Annunciation and Two Saints). Who
was Taddeo di Bartolo's model
for *St. Costanzo*? Considered Bonfigli's
fire-belching pigeon with burning feet
descending like a hood ornament,
shared a trifurcated pizza,
authored the red neon of five cigarettes.

Oh, we've also brought lots of mischief with us.
We've brought our Sherwin-Williams red paint
notions of breakfast and finesse to the bells

and well of summit Velsna. The modest shift
of a housewife is as Etruscan-familiar as old
names of Indian rivers. Arno, Tiber.
The dove disappears into a black square.

     *

The serenade of Vanth
is fugitive and red:

the horror and delight of the geranium
beneath a cemetery cyprus,

the drip of scarlet
oxidizing to a clot.

     *

Two glasses of wine are brought for your tasting. Once
you have tried each of them and selected your favorite,
the other is dutifully taken away. *Sopressatta*
under orange zest and oil, an array of meats
and cheese on toasted bread. The glasses sparkle.
A skull embedded in the wall of a rival city
still says: "I was once as you are now."

     *

Tonight jazzy "Helen of Troy" is carrying on
inside the aquarium-lit hotel front desk
cabana, the puffy bulimic face that launched
a thousand ships. In tonight's melodrama,

Velsna—the ancient Etruscan name for the present-day town of Orvieto.
Vanth—Etruscan goddess who would appear to meet and escort the re-
cently deceased to the underworld.

it is a half-dozen adulating adolescent
erections. Her "Domani!" to their "Oggi! Oggi!"

*

Perhaps wolves once lived in the spontaneous
vegetation of the Volsinii hills.
The miracle of a mother's love
still presides here.

We take pictures.
We savor the wine; the ham and sausage;
the vases; the continuity of the guises;

child in her
lap: dome: Vanth: Lupa: Queen of the Darkroom:
Our Lady of Sorrows.

Volsinii—the ancient name for the present-day district surrounding Or-
vieto.

American Cooking

French Service; Russian Service; Nouvelle Cuisine;
handmade array passed down, sometimes around

with grace. Honey, okra, watermelon,
black-eyed peas, and conduit of the Indian

fritter: deep-fried Arab falafel (Just who
decided the African eastern limit anyway?)

come home as southern hush puppy.
French fries, English chips, Saratoga

(these days, Hawaiian) crisps: revolving salty
American potato. Pecans and peanuts

for walnuts. Vanilla and cacao beans
for olives and dates; ancient sop

and Indian sugar; English grill, Dutch oven,
colonial fire. Washington ballasted his whiskey

with the sour delight of West Indian citrons.
Jefferson's palate, like that of sixteenth-century

Neapolitans, found pleasure in the delicate
acid of tomatoes in variety. Hunger,

native ingredients from the garden, and bound
recipes copied in the study by careful hands

continue their hope of savory and postprandial
port in a sweet and smoldering world.

Mene, Mene, Tekel, Upharsin

> They drank wine, and praised the gods of gold,
> and of silver, of brass, of iron, of wood, and of stone.
>
> —Daniel 5:4

Before entering one of the ancient gates
of Sienna's wall, we raise our eyes
to a modest art nouveau lintel decoration.
"Liberty prevails!" our friend reads. She
has seen and sees so much more than us:
something underlying the position of an urban
road; supplications picked out of the darkness,
scratched on paper; prayers brushed on cloth;
platelet offerings made according to a vow:
Mexican tin, Roman alloy, Russian silver.

In the cathedral, not the usual hands,
stomachs, and hearts—but a cluster
of flashy fiberglass motorcycle helmets
covering part of a wall stuns us:
modern expression just the other side
of an intrepid mother tongue.
Beneath the shiny surfaces,
schemata circulate around the chamber
inescapably seeking correlates.
Our fingers are warm and wet
without even touching a wound.

Bravado Farce

For E.M.

I have deliberately refrained
from introducing into our conversation
the controversy over the plans
to preserve the decrepit panopticon
over on Roosevelt Island,

the riddle of why it took until 1996
for the God-fearing voters of Mississippi
to ratify—with almost no fanfare—
the constitutional amendment
that brought an official end
to slavery here in the U.S.,

or my questions regarding
the stripping away of guises
and the last five stations of the cross.

Most of the signs and windows
above the intersection are harsh
in their brightness. Your tongue
glistens like a boxer's back,
though nothing in you smacks
of malice. For me, literally speaking,
this is dining high on the hog.

Over *Creative Foods for Home and Office*,
an Indian cotton block-print tree of life
bursts into bloom in someone's window.

Despite your squirming with urgency,
as we part you manage to grandly
yank the conversation up
like a prestidigitator's climactic
tablecloth: "We will solve it all!"

Amazing Grace

Richard Oswald's English respectability
was sustained by trading in—
among other things—human souls.
Twenty miles from the Saw of Lions' Teeth
(old familiar Sierra Leonean landmark,
majestic and haunting even to the Portuguese),
twenty miles from Freetown, a lush green isle,
furthest inland the trading ships
could go without running aground;
on its mysterious ramparts, cannons
to keep the marauding French away:
Bunce Island, with its lavish Georgian
manor, imitation gentry, formal gardens,
and Gullah-speaking rice farmers;
where someone's naked son, someone's
missing daughter, sat chained in circles
around practical troughs of rice.
Here, no one blew a horn. They slipped
through the gate; filed down to the jetty.

How many times had he cast his net
in nearby waters; how many times had she
gone with her grandmother and mother
to gather sweet grass for their baskets?
Had never heard of South Carolina
nor Charleston; neither, yet, John Newton's
soft refrain nor Henry Lawrence's name.

Contracted with what grace
might they have divined that one day,

miles and two hundred years later,
their lineage, obliged with Lawrence's
language, might find themselves free
to account names and read bitter instruments?

Spring Shearing

My grandfather ran a shearing crew; knew
how to pack, unpack, set up the flats; saw to it

that no shearing arm's oily teeth were ever far
from a dark tin snout luminous with amber.

My grandmother, then just a mother, would go
along and cook for the crew; among other things,

she made sure a burlap-wrapped canister
was set up clean and full of water. One season,

her hands were full with turkeys hatching.
My mother, barely a teenager, went in her stead

to cook in the tricky old Dutch oven. Coals
on top, coals below. She made sure there were,

among other things, a gold yeasty roll,
a drink, occasionally, an interval of relief

from the noise and deadeningly even vibrations.
Times that found the banal but powerful gasoline

engine shut down, the usual sounds and textures
of the world rebounded immediately: the air

and bending bones, stripped of their relentless
rippling mask, moved on. Among other things,

those hot and dusty days were about
a chore well done, even in those thirsty spells

of disorder which were but a span between
a contract and its fulfilled expectation.

A little salt, browned beef, tomatoes, onions,
beans, a little sugar. The well-fed crew jangled

tokens in their pockets; each one a claim
to a bleating head, nicked and shivering,

gangly and shorn; each portion of their
honor brought them one rung closer

to that chosen blue suit, to flour or
violet water for their belovéd. At night,

she dreamt; slept safely between her devoted
father and the peaceful, yellow-toothed rig.

In Visiting Hours

"Will you walk with me?"

Here no seeds are drying away
their sweet-smelling flesh in the window;
no thorny, air-bubble-covered rose stems
gently intertwine
like underwater ballerinas in fruit jars;

no jelly jars, pink Depression glass,
or other survivors of sets long broken,
casually assembled,
are turned upside-down on clean shelf paper.

"I've brought you lotion and talc."

The ugly patterned fabric has been pinned
across where her breasts used to be,
the sweater buttons unaligned.

"What should I do now?"

Much like those first moments
sitting in the seat of a tandem disk-pulling tractor;
how keeping my eyes on that establishing point
assures me my rows are being cut
the way I want them.

"Yesterday I visited with Aunt Ladell.
And today . . . I spoke with Aunt Opal. . . .
Opal." As if that sororal familiarity
might come from some place deeper
than any tranquilizer could reach.

"Berley?" She thinks that I am . . .
my father, her favorite. Am I prepared
unexpectedly to fill the absence?
Strange, her cloudy precision.

"Will you walk with me?
What shall I do now?"

Here spinach and cornbread come in putty-colored
Melmac on stackable turquoise plastic trays,
the little tumblers are plastic, the furniture
is screwed together, the lighting, of industrial design.

"I've got to go. I love you."

With our mouths and ears still
closely positioned, the delicate fingers
on my cheek instruct me to linger,
and much to my surprise

we are both returning
to that familiar unoccupied point.

Fortune-Telling

We waited on the porch:
benches and chairs cushioned
in a provincial flower print.

A hollyhock bush (*Althaea rosea*),
larkspur, and roses bloomed the full
length of the modest veranda.

Our visit with Mrs. Griffay took
the better part of a day. "Tea?"
She studied the pattern

clinging dregs made in the saucer,
her eyes moving across the cup's
bottom and inner wall.

Mrs. Griffay, a small, unassuming
woman (bun at her crown)
resembled my great-grandmother,

Althea Pearl Duncan Harbour.
Her dress—made of the same fabric
as covered the cushions on the porch.

Mom found out she and Dad
would be adding on to the house
in *both* directions. My gypsy feet

would take me to distant lands
more than once. Mrs. Griffay
was fondest of reading

for my sister. Hers were
the longest sessions, though
it was my mother and brother

who were keenest on the visits.
I wondered about botanical
families. According to Webster,

hollyhock was a Chinese herb.
Where marshmallow (*Althaea
officinalis*, "whose roots were used

in confectionery and medicine")
was a European herb. Both
were in the mallow family. Perhaps

my great grandmother had been born
in the shade of a hollyhock bush.
Perhaps a Chinese family had

stopped in Europe before ending up
in Mrs. Griffay's yard in Texas.
Later, in my travels, I would search

the faces of the fortune-tellers
of Valentin, Caravaggio,
Manfredi, La Tour, David.

Rhythm and Blues: Rings and Burls

> . . . the dark opening to admit us . . . less personal
> but no less tender.
>
> —Mark Doty

I've been back to visit the deep, black banks
Of the scraggly creek. The two hollows of trees
And the woods and grassy pastures still fade
Into one another. A man and a local
Child made maps and notes for the awkward other.

Polio took neighbors and neighbors' children.
AIDS and opportunistic infections took closest
Friends and a brother. The young men rowing
Of Eakins grow familiar. What's difficult once
You've gotten started is how to keep on going.

Festival

Before the restaurant's large garden window,
after the holiday feast, a single coffee
at the uncleared table. Dieffenbachia,
white poinsettia, Chinese evergreen,
and mother-in-law-tongues habituate
where the names of native trees have never grown.

What if the Christ child had been a girl,
growing through her youth: desert wanderer:
whose mother prays for her as she founds
her ministry and finds her destiny
unfurling into fulfillment of the law?

It's beginning to look a lot like the festival
of divine principals leaving the mythical
and coming into the mortal affair
of history. It's the seasonal aisle
of sundry at the drugstore: ENTRANCE,
the colorful bookend of Easter,
the exit marked in red.

        *

In sober paint on canvas, on the day
of a believer's death, a row of mourning heads
underlies an infant passing into the joy
of real justice, divine estate, a moving
landscape of pure unmoving love.
Clearly, El Greco and others in Toledo
and of his era were absolute with their metaphors.

        *

Several wads of wrapping paper
crumpled on a corner table
glitter like torch flames reflected
in the mirrored headdresses
of elephants carrying a local god.

Each spring, South India
blooms with celebrations:
operas, Kathakali, fireworks.

Each year, deities routinely
journey out of their respective houses
to the banks of a river to be bathed
or to a barge in a river to pass a night
with their respective consorts.
Each of them, likewise, has left behind
a holy precinct.

The vehicles of the corteges
(musicians and priests
with swishing manes, lolling fans,
and gold dangling-disk-edged canopies)—
both leaving and homing—are elephants.
Everyone comes out to play
in the presence of the deities
and their vehicles. Fireworks
fill the late night sky.

        *

Semana Santa in Andalusia.
The *paso* and *cofrodia* return to their church.

---

paso—a float carrying a religious icon.
cofrodía—a societal order or congregation.

50

A *saeta* drops from an unlit balcony
as the bearers gradually rock

the *paso* in and out:
a lullaby. In and out. In.

The only youngster in our party
is completely tuckered out.

As our group, heads quietly together,
finally ambles home together,

Horacio and I take turns carrying
dreaming Maria through the streets.

---

saeta—literally "arrow"; in Andalusia, a hymn of a pierced heart.

With an Instinctive Certainty of the Charms of the Modish, "For the Fairest"

It doesn't look like western Turkey
to me. It looks more like the towns
and citadels of the craggy
north; more like the light of Germany;
        like the early sixteenth
century. Elegant, well bred,
alert; cool, naked, probably
perfumed. Horizontal
repetitions of heads, arms, hands, navels,
        knees, and feet scroll down
the picture plane.

        The tree—back up
at the top—one big diagonal,
seems both to secure
and set off the prince's horse who, if
        he cannot see them as we
do, clearly senses their presence.
He seems alarmed.

        Apparently,
the one in the gold
armor is the only one the prince
        so far can see. He is
watching his fair mouth.

        Hermes may be
explaining everything from

the beginning, why in
the first place Zeus allowed Eris to attend
                    the ceremony.

                But my guess is that he has
                chosen the more expedient
course. Something more along
the lines of profit-motive, like ". . . as re-
                    warding as pressing grapes.
                A goddess can be quite liberal
                if not downright generous;
indirectly, down-
right generous, if you know what I mean."
                    His right hand wraps
                around his sword and makes a fist more
                horizontal than a codpiece.
The horse's eyes and nose
seem vaguely reminiscent of the prince;
                    vaguely reminiscent of
                that tiny spout of water that
                rings the puddle just under
the prince's stone perch; a kind
of nervous tremor which, as it crosses
                    the canvas, converts in
                the rhythm of the deathless limbs.
                In a few more moments, he will
see them as clearly as
we do: those locks of untressed golden hair,
                    the pale and sinuous
                lines their bodies make against
                the writhing curtain of tendrils,
shadowy and green;
a tapestry; goddesses in bloodless
                    guises. Not born. More trans-
                ferred in, like ink through a silk screen;
                like a Marilyn, an

Elizabeth, a Jacqueline;
the star, the conquering Egyptian legend,
                    the queen in a pink pill-
                box hat or widow's weeds. Long legs
                and delicate limbs; slender to
the point of leanness; small
breasts, no full curves except their protruding
                        stomachs. Dreamy; outlines with
                minimal interior drawing
                or modeling. All chokered, jeweled,
coiffed, and chained; draped in cloth
that looks to me like cellophane. Do you
                        see how the unbroken,
                localized color and light
                weld light to shade, forest to sky?
Only the goddesses
stand out. Two turn their eyes away from
                        us. The one on the left
                props her pale right arm across
                Hermes's armored back like the single
exposed blade of a knife
opened above the smooth, gently commingled
                        contours of their sides.
                The cocked, wide-brimmed, red velvet hat of
                the other with Paris's cocked,
wide-brimmed, plumed, red velvet hat
brackets the scene. Her left arm lines against
                        her body like the blood
                groove of a knife. They turn their eyes
                toward the figure in the middle.
She exhibits herself
to us with a goddess's instinctive
                        certitude. She holds her
                wrists back, servile and opaque, as
                if submitting herself to man-
acles. Her eyes engage

with ours. What a peculiar place to
                    find ourselves expected,
                unexpected specificity.

                This is a peculiar place
well prepared by Lucas
Cranach, ingeniously crafted by his mind's
                    living, clever, clear eye.

Currency at the "Common Ground"

The proprietors of our upstate bed
& breakfast are our guides to this *neck*
of the woods tonight. Kathy & Linda
snuggle in their chairs behind us;
gleefully steal a kiss. For some,
the shimmering, onstage illusions
are just half a day away from the bright
industrial light of a nine-to-five
in a discount-store aisle. Another
week and we will be prowling
the shimmering green canopy
above the ancient Arab baths of Ronda.

The display, here—a cosmetic tear
glittering on the face of Kitty Litter
or Barb Bitchuate—is partially
made up of praise, the old language
of lyric gesture, and the possession
of a knowledge not much prized.
A condemned woman—here,
tonight, in Ithaca, raising her face
and hands toward the sky—
implores mercy, booms, dazzles,
contracts. The pathos of the man
beneath the diva's makeup
blooms. This gathering is not
about playing to win. Bills
rustle—some themselves offerings

just taken by other performers;
in turn, openly bestowed, along
with the tuck of an acknowledging look,
the genuine tribute of a modest kiss.

Yasumasa Morimura as Frida Kahlo

Luhring Augustine Gallery, N.Y.C., 2001

St. Francis doesn't see her coming. He is preoccupied
with the enigmatic adjuration playing in his head.
We know he is heading toward the full-scale
renunciation in the village square
and the rest of his life repairing
a rough tunic. But today the mania swirls
like bolts of his father's rich and luxuriant fabric.
From his upper-story window, he finds
each unfurling as radiant as a lily.

Yasumasa Morimura is below. He sees
her: white roses completely encircle
her face, and a tiny silver cross
dangles down to the center of her forehead
from a pair of opened pale yellow roses.
Her hair, completely covered.
Her dress, made entirely of white lace.
She seems engulfed in white out to the edges
of her icy-sparkling fern-radiating
headdress. Somber as an Aztec.
Static as a Byzantine. Starched as a Catholic
icon. Singular as a word: "Revolución."

As another avatar, she clutches a nosegay
in her right hand. Embroidered flowers
completely cover her red dress. Pink
and red flowers and a ribbon of red
braid into a crown with her hair. She wears

a gaggle of colorful bangles on her wrists.
Her elbow swings like a hinged shutter. She
wears a pronounced old-world red cabochon ring
on one finger of her left hand. It closes over her heart. Opens
out to her side when she says, "Lo odio!"
It rises sharply up and further back than her shoulder.
"Mi chiquito lindo." The woman of feelings.
"Te amo más que a mi misma."

And another guise. Her hair is swept up
and tied. On top of her head, a big red bow
accents the bright red dress. A saffron shawl
drapes cross her lap. Both face and fingernails painted.
A large gold ring on each hand, and gold bracelets.
She carrys a bright red flag on a gold staff.
The flag face has a gold glyph on it.
"Enfrenta el dolor!" "Estoy triste."
[laughter] "Qué chistoso." . . . "'Ayúdame."

And Morimura as Yasumasa Morimura,
the man evoking Frida, sits on a bench at a keyboard.
Gutterals sometimes elicit Kabuki. The keyboard
sometimes elicits the notes of a Japanese samisen.
Morimura elicits Kahlo. It's a video,
so he can portray and interchange all of the guises.

Lo odio!—I hate him!
Mi chiquito lindo—My little precious one
Te amo más que a mi misma—I love you more than my own self
Enfrenta el dolor!—Face the pain!
Estoy triste—I am sad
Qué chistoso—How amusing
Ayúdame—Help me

John Kelly
as Dagmar Onassis
as Joni Mitchell

September 7, 1992,
Tompkins Square Park, N.Y.

The *WIGSTOCK*s behind you
psychedelically balloon on canvas

in unapologetic yellow on hot pink
on yet another paler pink.

A polite cluster of real
orange and blue balloons

off to the side
(from our perspective, behind you)

seems to be patiently awaiting ascent.
A diva in a short dress and a blond wig;

lithe fingers in long black gloves.
We can see that your arms and legs

are lean (cut from the same material),
that your face is painted,

and that you carry a piece
of sparkling, sheer, red cloth—

bright, alarming, and fugitive:
Speller of the Park.

Above and behind you, birds,
trees, and evening clouds intersect.

You warble, ". . . we've got
to get ourselves back to the garden."

Off the Hook

You and I sit on the couch and confess
our blunders, how we have gamboled up to others
wanting to say, "You are entirely lovable"—
but, instead, have drowned

that simple affirmation in the water
with, "I come to you dressed as the old dull
knife-drag of desire." You and I sit on the couch
and play several rounds

of "Hangman." Your hands keep drawing gibbets
with tiny hooks. Your words keep turning
into burning wings of birds. The subject
skips and glints. You feel

that separate passions—in the covenant
between two men—are capricious, dangerous,
objectionable. I lose with "commerce." You win
with "ort" and "certainty."

Fortune Three

I keep coming back to you and you, and you to each
other. Friendship rises, fans out, seeks a place it can
anchor without fear. One of us has had too much
to drink. Another has

genteelly walked someone else home, given us
the slip. The integer is broken and nothing
either of us can do can keep our craft from rocking.
Strange our hungry ghost of love.

Each, an entity at work, we walk. I admire
but say nothing about the seven white tulips perky
as swords. It is night. A bitter tempest simmers
in your wobbly pot,

"My point here. . . ." As if evoked, the dapper object
of our agitation strides out of the dappling shadow
of a tulip tree. Shoes. Up: cuffs, hands, chest,
the familiar smile.

Yes, you've found your goat and lamb ambling shoulder
to shoulder. Obliging no transformation of victim
to enemy, we grasp the meaning of tendering
without the taste of lash.

Dim Sum in Philadelphia

Our hostess translates it for us: "a little
tug at the heart." Like me, she knows
about sliding down to single syllables.
At the table next to ours,

a couple feeds their toddler with chopsticks.
You, calm and relaxed, smile, reflect,
and (somewhat unexpectedly) express
how they remind you

of a family of birds. But I know you
are preoccupied with the mental health
of your long-time friend now living
in San Francisco. You

are better with the body. I should know;
you've been my secret for twenty years.
Your posture is a familiar countenance:
the pattern of a migration

in a dream. Many nights, I've lain aside
your shirt, white, formal, consenting.
You brought your subtleties to our table
in the city; I,

my brashness, and a drawl. You came watchful
of the forest; I, the bush. Our tracks hazard
in the dune, trusting: the appearance of a file
will hide our number,

that the wind will erase our words; a turning
wheel of stars, our time together. The coast,
for now, is clear of everything but a constancy
of being watched and wanted.

Four Saints in Three Acts:

The Company of Mark Morris

> . . . 'heaven: stern,
> Very clean, virtuous and a little dull . . .
> —Erin Belieu, "Choose Your Garden"

seven playful couples
worthy of one another

circle and couple:
Miss Stein . . . Mr. Thomson:

a tangerine-peach sky
with magpies

hovers over a cherry-blossom pink,
rose-colored-glasses background

(orange juice floating on grenadine):
Loyola's tan—a picturesque *tall*

drink of water with a sparkling
silver cross on his downy chest:

the corresponding pattern
of a faint sun and snowflake

appears (white on white)
on his cumber bun

and her baby doll:
his white Spanish pants

are long to the knee
sans grass stains:

her gown does not even
start to cover her legs:

each of the six young fisherboys
has a different-colored handkerchief

around his neck: Teresa's
ungathered white dress

is very short; like her, the girls
all wear small silver crosses:

all the gaiety of flamenco,
none of the sadism of a tango:

fabulous as a swing,
not a playground cone pole,

but something more individual
the kind you would drop

from a tree in spring:
nothing harsh or fugitive:

just as erotically
insistent as all

the coupling
circling and recoupling:

a few orchestrated minutes
of cavorting in paradise

Salgado's *Two Men in a Sauna*

Two dark triangles: supportive elbow
to supportive elbow. The pose evokes Michelangelo's

Nightfall & Dawn or *Nightfall* and *Day*;
only, here, in a Ukrainian metallurgical workers' sauna,

no broken marble plinth separates you.
One coy wrist. We've seen that groin touching before—

in countless Renaissance illuminations, lamentations,
entombments, choreographies on marble graves.

The lifeless droop, expired or vital,
renders a judgment

(the way a dead Christ on the cross
averts his head from the bad thief).

Palpable reality fondled, taken in the hand,
receives a wound. First wound,

first shedding of blood, the self-touching
hand, the groin-searching hand;

a cupping hand
points back to the beginning.

Whether the mother, the father, the living
Godhead, or the sovereign corpse itself; passion

mortally approaches perfection;
likewise, here, in the casual gesture made

by one of two men
framed in sanctified space.

April 11, 1861, Arrowhead

I am back
        from Washington. Back
    to the old troubles, and troubles
    there are. The poems are a pale,
unsalvageable disaster; though, like the weather,
    nothing a good fire can't
    take care of.
            Seeing you again was
an unexpected pleasure. Of late, I have
        spent too many months alone
    silently drifting. I have watched no
triumphant procession massing from a sea
        of blurry pages; have
    floundered beneath a fading reef
of distant faces. What a delight to find
        your familiar confidence
    floating above me again; to find
myself lifted and warmed by your affection.

    I am enclosing one of *my* recent
    photographs. Here, rather than tamped
into a clown's guise, you will find my "Dutch-cut,"
        though framed in the posture of
    a mummy, no less solicitous of love.
Accept this in exchange for the lovely cards.

    You have already heard
    my story of wandering before
the marmoreal Piazza Novona
        and my later impressions
    standing before those extraordinary
treasures of the Vatican Museum.

That spectacular torso
was, beyond a doubt, my favorite.

Mr. Lincoln was charming. One might
        Even note, subtly handsome . . .
or oddly—dare I write it?—salacious.
As you suggested, I also met Ward Lamon
        and John Hay and found both
true to your description. Lamon,
though no Apollo, is indeed a husky beauty.

        Thank you again both for
the lovely photographs and for all
your kindnesses in Washington. Should you
        find yourself near Pittsfield,
know there is always a fire for you
at Arrowhead. Besides cigars and brandy,
        you will find my pine chariot
and my whip at your disposal.
I would be happy to treat you to a drive.
        We could go either up to
Greylock or, as I am more inclined,
down to Stockbridge, to Monument Mountain
        and the mysterious, licentious
shade of Ice Glen. Come. I remain yours,
tinged with a certain gratitude. Herman M.

Dignity at "Trumpets"

"The Declaration of Independence,
Bill of Rights, and Constitution
are all here, not far away, in high
security vaults of extraordinary design."

My friend then orders Bacardi Limón
in her fine *cubano* accent. If the city
were overtaken by a disaster, our most
valued political documents would await—

locked in their dignity—new readers.
I'm still with the shower-whipped roses
we sloshed by on our way from the sessile
Dupont Circle Station maw: Odysseus

and his men sailing away from Death's Island,
and Aeneas and Dante finding their way
after their dialogues in worlds without
art; each a past informing the day . . .

One of our tablemates, a nurse, is finishing
his story. The denouement: at the end
of a journey, a youth faces his grandfather
for the first time in a bodega in Salinas, P. R.

Secrecies are most often despicable. Five
private missions edify one train of thought:
"It is a privilege to educate,
it is a privilege to heal."

Traveler

The bounded is loathed by its possessor.
The same dull round, even of a universe,
would soon become a mill with complicated wheels.
　　　　—William Blake, "There Is No Natural Religion"

The fevers of the dying are wooded
with animals we'll never know.

We sleep near one another
in starlight that radiated out

years before the fragrant
scallions of Ashkelon,

before the syncopations
of the first poem

or the invention of the sentence
(celestial hand puppet),

incandescent haunt,
deeper than retina—

wave and particle,
arrow

made out of onions,
arrow

made out of string.

En la fuente de las conchas, en el Paseo del Prado, Madrid

June 6, 1990

In Memoriam Aurora de Albornoz

Picasso's *Bull* with specks of foxing
and rustling wings has come

from behind the glass and frame.
In clear and warming sunlight,

he has come from behind the front door
of her apartment on Calle Méjico

to the fountain's splashing water
to drink. He snorts in Sapphic metrics,

unprotected; no longer restrained
by one of her hands, small and spotted

like a bunting. The warming sunlight
moves up the poet's light stone amber leg.

Though the pitted and shadowy glyphs
are inconsistent . . . their message is not.

It reads: "Death. Death has come
and found me. Wrap me in a clean

white cloth and bury me
in Luarca. Better yet,

burn me and bury my ashes
in Puerto Rico by the sea."

Tartessos

—Rhys Carpenter, *Greeks in Spain*, 1925

One day in their city in the Bay of
                Smyrna where it
        has been said the climate is
perhaps the most
beautiful in the whole world, fifty-odd
                Phocaean men
        went down and set out in their
longship. They would
cross the Aegean with its island step-
                ping stones, round the
        southern cape of Greece and sail
up the western
shores of Peloponnesus, Epirus,
                and Corcyra.
        They would cross to the heel of
Italy and,
in their second week of seafaring, pass
                through the fearful
        Sicilian straits. Still coasting
a Grecian shore,
they would come to the Bay of Naples and
                to ancient Cumae
        and Ischia, which they called
Pithekussa—
"Monkey Island." Here they would abandon
                their preference
        for hugging the shore and, af-
ter skirting the

Ponza Islands, they would sail the next
                    sixty miles in the
            shelterless, unharvestable,
open sea. At
Olbia, on that old island bridge *we*
                    call Sardinia,
            they would prepare once more.
After Ichnussa
(what *they* called Sardinia) there would be
                    Melussa,
            Kromyussa, the Pityussae,
and Ophiussa.

These emerging -*ussa* endings, if taken
                    as a route, form
            a perfect track to that
mysterious
Hesperian land of ocean and western
                    trade wind where
            it was said, in the strange lands
beyond the gates
of Hercules, strange rivers flow
                    through marshes,
            the nights are short,
the mysterious shores
are rich with fog and chthonic shrines;
                    the land of the
            Laestrygons, near where it
must have been that,
sailors said, Medusa had grown her reef
                    of heads, near where
            it must have been that Atlas
held up the sky.

The Garum Pits of Baelo

Not far above the converging point of Tarifa,
the white walls of Bolonia lightly hunker in
a little upland from the Atlantic tides.
Isabel's SUV has sped us here between
the ranges of La Plata and San Bartolomé.
In the ancient world, this was a busy port,
a center famous for the manufacturing of *garum*
(the way, for a moment, some tribes of native Amerinds
industriously harvested orchards of peaches).
Southwestern tomatoes, eastern oranges, commuters,
and computers have all found their way here,
prime ingredients to sauces of later empires.
Though no orange trees grow here. No trees at all,
and we've left our laptop back in San Roque.
How the endless swelling and dropping
must have perplexed the Mediterranean sailors.
Above its bluffs, white twirling blades
of turbines bluster the intercontinental
migration of winds and birds.

The uninterrupted Baeloian tides were
ancient even before the ranging tones
of the rock-cut *garum* pits' two millennia.

We wonder if these pits predate
the tanning vats of Fez; speculate
on the lives of giant basket weavers.
It must have been much the same
process as Phoenician murex extraction:
"Break the shell, extract the fish,
and deposit it in the vats where the dye

liquefies out. As it putrefies, it will
secrete a yellowish liquid which provides—

according to the strength used—
tones ranging from rose to dark
violet. For the darker tones,
exposure to the sun is necessary.
Best to have the 'factory' on the lee side
of the town, as the odors are not pleasant."

A ramshackle church, a cabana restaurant,
two site-attending archeologists, and a cat
are the modern inhabitants of Baelo
Claudia of Bética, with her once proposing
theatre and her once inviting baths.

Cusp and Tether

The exquisitely laced, perfect ball
leaves an acetylene-blue trail in the air.

Eros and Ganymede play together
on the ground like Jesus and John.

The most elaborate of Zeus's boyhood
cosmic toys is drawn from the safe

to bait incorrigible
Eros. (It's an old trope;

though, here—instead of the old
divinities in new disguises—

Apollonius's radical new style
puts human charity on trial.)

A nurse made the toy
while living in jeopardy

in the Idaean cave.
Medea tosses and turns;

her inner world shimmers like light
reflecting off churning water

or a planet. (One by one
we sense a turning

from Gilgamesh or Homer
toward Gethsemane.)

Apollonius has Jason toss
himself into the fray

like a blazing heavenly body
three hundred years before

the incarnate infant Christian god's
glimmering star.

And today on the train,
a young scribbler

records a toy vender
moving between cars.

The hot selling battery-powered
yo-yo flashes and blinks—

delights, winding
and rewinding on its string.

Tacking

You call and let me know that you've been
distracted; ask how my day has been,
what I am doing. Can I wrap up the last
books of the *Iliad* and join you for a movie?
You choose something with "indemnity"
or "verdict" in its title.
                              Later, when you
ask if I was rooting for the prosecution
or the defense, I blanch.

    *

                              Another day;
another call. This time I'm rereading
the *Odyssey*. You choose something
with a sensational chase scene.
In the end, a diligent man clapped
another into handcuffs and wandered off
into the credits. You winced, leaned over,
and said you would have liked a frozen frame
with a simple caption at the end. I whisper,
". . . And Penelope said, 'You've come back.'"

    *

                              We stay in; talk,
cook, and take in *Golden Oldies* on TV.
You, feeling guilty for not working through
your tower of medical journals, pipe up
that boredom is a presentation of anxiety.
I've enjoyed the evening. But, then again,
I have been reading Theocritus

and the second movement of *The Waste Land*
and wondering about songbirds
and if the golden fleece
had any power left when it ceased
to mark the holy center of a world.

Cathedral Plaza

Santiago de Compostela

Out of the decorated tower on
                        the right, the clank
            and clash of bells like a pair
of dull, broad blades
engaging in the brisk air of morning
                        sound. The last bell
            dilapidates
to its final
clap: a flat, slow stone skipping on a
                        cold, still pond;
            a shoed hoof on hard terrain.
A new sun radiates,
no clouds. The light, cool wind is a kind
                        of elixir.
            With eyes closed, I course in an
infinite but
uninhabitable, incandescent
                        field of red branches.
            Yesterday, the curious
red instrument
suspended at the end of someone's giant
                        crane resembled
            Santiago's cross. In to-
day's light and o-
verriding breeze, fugitive distractions
                        radiantly burn
            themselves through blood and flesh
almost to gold.